Reflections and Other Poems

Reflections and Other Poems

Albert M. Juergens, Jr.

Huntersfield Mountain Press

Reflections and other Poems by
Albert M. Juergens, Jr.

Published by Huntersfield Mountain Press,
Prattsville, NY 12468

Illustrated by
John A. Dooley
Angela M. Schmied

Library of Congress catalog card number
92-075912

ISBN 0-9635010-0-3

Contents

REFLECTIONS

Reflections

What is it we remember? The
Good, the traumatic, the evil?
To relate, yes. But what of that
Which makes us? The non-relatable,
The feeling which warms; the contrast
Of the cold white harshness of a
Winter's day with the permeating
Golden glow of an open fire; the
Shuddering slap on the back from
The old friend, long not seen;
The soft stroke of a caress from
A lover never absent. All tempering
And forming, still forgotten in the
Tempest of doing, achieving, dying.

* * *

The dirt path was worn hard, bordered
By stubbly grass, fighting against
Footsteps for existence. The man
Walked slowly, looking straight ahead,
Unmindful of the small boy's hand
Wrapped around his finger, or the
Occasional glance affirming in the
Immature mind the connection
Of the finger to the person.
For awhile the boy kept up, taking
Three steps to each two, but then lagged.
The man sensed the effort of the boy;
Looking down, he smiled, then
Lifted him up and carried him.

* * *

The bus was gigantic, the sudden burst
Of compressed air as it stopped, explosive
On his ears. He saw the driver lean to
Push the silver colored lever handle,
Opening the doors. He forgot his mother
As the doors closed behind him, and he
Seemed to float down the isle until he spotted
An empty seat, its shiny brown leather
Stiff and hard. He was unaware of the eyes
Studying him, his interest was caught by
The oval handle grip located on each double seat.
The bus stopped, he saw the school building,
Then followed the children's rush to embark,
Unknowingly entering a world unknown.

* * *

The rain had fallen for three days.
Water would ooze up from the sponge
Rendered lawn to cover the rim of
Leather sole with each step, then
Disappear as the grass sprang back
To fill the footprint. The boy jumped
Over the puddle formed by the sinking of
A sidewalk square, and ran into the house.
The wind increased from gusting to a
Steady rush, only slowing to concentrate
It's effort into greater force. The rain
Restarted, driven in a horizontal slash,
Penetrating the window's seams, creeping
Upward on their inner surface.

The branches of the willow strained
Outward, trying to whip the house in
Frustration, lacking shelter, desperately
Presenting an ever smaller silhouette
For the wind to target, yet howling
As the air ripped through it, slowly
Bending its trunk, until with a sigh
It stretched, reclining, its uprooted
Base naked to the sky. The boy peered
Through the tearing eye of a window,
Wondering at what unseen hand could
Render a tree helpless, cause fear
To darken the face of a mother, fire
A father's eyes with anger.

* * *

The girl stood, her eyes not seeing,
Sight overwhelmed by the power of thought,
Observed by the boy, astride his
Stilled bicycle, baseball mitt hanging,
Forgotten, from the handlebar. From a
Distance of a half street width, he studied
The slender figure, the blonde hair
Pulled back from the delicate face, while
Within, the first pangs of a new
Sense disturbed the tranquillity of
Boyhood. As she turned, her gaze halted
A moment, catching his stare. A flash
Of heat reddened him, as his eyes dropped,
Confused, wondering what had been wrong.

* * *

The powder-like dust eddied as their
Sneakered feet struck the sun baked road.
His jeans stuck, sweat stained, to his
Thighs. The rising dust dissolved in
Little tricklets marking their paths as
They coursed down her bare ankles to her
Sockless feet. He tried not to look at
Her wet soaked shirt, soiled by her
Wiping her face, clinging to her
Swelling chest, taut over its pinnacles
Of pink, which she had carelessly exposed
While cooling herself, revelling in his
Discomfort. He fought the compulsion to
Reach out and touch her. She laughed.

The swallows flitted nervously in the
Grey dark under the barn roof, worried at the
Intrusion. She climbed ahead of him, her
Bare feet curling around the polished
Rungs of a ladder set into beams, hewn
By hands of a farmer long gone, upward
To where she could jump to the top of
The newly stored hay, still sweet with
Sunshine. He followed, trying not to see
Her legs flexing gently within nut brown
Skin, fading to an ivory as it disappeared
Beneath the frayed cloth of her shorts,
While his body pulsated between strength and
Weakness, anticipating the unknown.

A force tried to draw him to her, as she
Reclined, playing with a reed of hay,
Rolling it in her fingers, stroking it over her
Lips, biting at it with her straight white teeth.
She was talking, but he didn't hear.
Within him a welling urge to encompass
And caress her was being weakly controlled
By the restraint of convention, a confusion
Ruled by don't, baseless, lacking reason,
Yet effective because of incomplete knowledge.
Her shorts loosely draped below her waist
Exposed her navel, and the taut skin over
Her pelvic structure beckoned. "My mother's
Calling. I've got to go." He left.

The cool poured from the mountain, filling
The evening with fragrance distilled from
The hot summers day. As others talked, she
Came to him. "Walk with me?" They left.
He found her hand in his. "I wish I could
Count the stars." He watched her eyes as
They swept the heavens. "Why?" "To know
What I don't know." "What good is that?"
She smiled as she looked at him. "Maybe
Knowing something would make me happy."
He felt quivering within his body. Impulses
Trying to escape, colliding in confusion.
The moon cast the shadow of an oak at
Their feet. A dog barked in the valley.

Her black braided hair was crowning her
Head, held in place by a shell comb. Her
Halter dress open in the back, exposed to
His mind, tawny skin, crisscrossed with bands,
Untouched by the sun's rays. The essence of
Perfumed soap was gently propelled by the
Warmth of her body, surrounding him, as he
Wished he could surround her. She faced him,
Her dark eyes looking into his. "You don't
Understand, do you?" "Understand what?"
She didn't answer, continuing to look into
His eyes, seeing the bewilderment of innocence.
"Tomorrow I go. When I'm gone, I'll think
of you." She pulled his face to hers.

* * *

The water slipped in an unending silver
Ribbon over the crest of the dam, silently
Separate from the roar of the billows
Frothing below in boiling fury, celebrating
Freedom from the granite constraint,
Sending mists hued with rainbows heavenward,
An offering to be momentarily bemused by
The reformed river; forgetful; unthinking.
The tons of falling water vibrates the
Ground on which he stands, dazed,
Gazing on the unending flow, unable to
Comprehend the power, the action of a
Raindrop, multiplied to a trickle,
Compounded to a reflection of God.

* * *

The classroom was hot with the late
September heat. Through the open
Window he looked down on the gymfield
Across the street, bordered with a
Cyclone fence which seemed to rise from
The discarded debris caught on its base.
The blue uniformed female bodies were
Moving like ants, their pattern perhaps
Only Intelligible to themselves or
Their teacher, who would blow her
Whistle while gesturing commands, which
If heeded, made little difference to
The activity he observed. After Waterloo
Napoleon was exiled to St. Helena.

The excited yelps of the girls voices, the
Sound of the whistle and the heat drew
His mind to the beach, the white sand tinged
With grey shadows, hot and squeaky under
His feet as he walked, mindful of the
Sanddust plume which followed each step,
Yet careless to where it struck, proceeding
To the water, thumping against the sand,
Spraying its delightful salty mist into
The air, then receding, leaving strips of
Bubbly foam stranded on the now glistening,
Now dull wet caked shoreline. He felt the
Crack of cold as he dove through the wave.
Napoleon died May 5, 1821.

* * *

The ground beneath his back was still warm
From the sun of the day. The grass of the dried
Lawn was stiff, crackling under the weight of his
Head. As his eyes accommodated the darkness of
The sky, stars became apparent in ever increasing
Numbers. Pinholes in the envelope of night.
Even as he tried to count, more droplets of
Light would surround the field, twinkling on,
Uncertain at first, then stronger, until he
Realized the futility of the count. He became
Conscious of his breathing, as he grew aware
Of the nothingness between his being
And stars, an abyss, incalculable, with
No reference point, endless, overwhelming.

* * *

The bright red of her glistening raincoat
Clashed with the off-copper red of her
Hair, loosely curling out from beneath
The hood. Her books were clutched to
Her body, their soggy condition unnoticed
As she gazed dreamily down the street,
Her green eyes hued with purple, unseeing.
He watched her from the car window, the
Rain flecks joining on the glass into
Water strings to play with his view,
Illuminating her image with light
Refracted from the grey autumn sky.
Her lips, now smiling, now pouting,
Called to his unwakened passion.

He was alone, no one would hear, yet
A knot was building in his stomach.
He picked up the receiver, and started to
Dial, only to stop and replace the
Phone in its cradle. What if she
Didn't answer? What would he say to
Her father? Maybe her mother would
Answer. Just ask if she's there.
Simple. But complex. Dial.
Busy. Dial. Busy. Who is she
Talking to? Perhaps making a date.
He would be refused. Dial. Busy.
Confrontation reduces ungrounded fear.
With relief, the phone was ringing.

Was the night warm? Outside their metal
Cocoon, submerged in the soft black
Nothingness, contrasted only by the
Moth infested glare of a streetlight,
The only reality was the occasional sound
Of an automobile passing on the street below.
He didn't remember her moving, yet he was
Holding her in his arms, her face looking
Up at his, her smiling lips glistening
In the faintly reflective light. His hands
Felt the curvature of her ribs, his mind
Struggled to comprehend her closeness; compact,
Complete, belonging; leaping from the physical
A yearning for eternity, unchanging foreverness.

A march was being played as they filed into the
Auditorium, walking awkwardly up onto the stage,
Where the sweltering closeness of the classmates
Mitigated the embarrassment of attention. He saw
His mother, smiling, perhaps witnessing the
Culmination of another step of motherhood
Relieved at its successful conclusion. At her side
His father, straight, absent, perhaps reminiscing
On differences of life then as viewed from now.
His view shifted to the girl next to his parents.
She was watching him, yet vibrant in her own
Existence, her eyes sparkling, her being
Crackling with that force which drew him to her,
Uncontrolled, indiscreet, exciting, powerful.

The celebration was over, they were alone, their
World defined by the beam of the headlights as
They drove. She slouched in the corner of the seat
Watching him with a studying look, while his
Eyes would flit from the road to caress her image,
Like the beam of a lighthouse light, revolving,
Reaching out, wanting to be protective from a
Distance. Protect or possess? Or a recognition,
Seminal in form, that man is incomplete in his
Stand-alone gender, missing forces necessary to
Complete the life journey, and when those forces
Are recognized, a desire to possess, protect,
Isolate and engulf them for ones own. A need
Fulfilled by surrender and incorporation.

The day on the boat had been warm, but now
In the rumble seat the air seemed cold as
The car sped over the darkened road. He could
See her hair quivering in the wind by the
Red glow of the tail lights. The occasional
Blip of light as they passed under streetlights
Illuminated her face. Underneath the lap
Blanket, her leg was pressed against his. His
Hand contacted the bare skin of her thigh, causing
A flash of heat within his body. She put her
Hand on his, pausing for a moment as their
Eyes met, then reluctantly forced his hand
Away, her taut skin slipping under his fingertips
Smooth, warm, inviting, desirable, forbidden.

* * *

The Cabin John-Glen Echo streetcar screeched
As it turned from 36th to Prospect below his
Window, he stared at the light reflected
On his room ceiling, alone, wondering; a
Million thoughts fighting for recognition
Within his head, his body relaxed on the
Starched sheet covered surplus Army bed, his
Spirit reviewing possibilities which might
Arise in the future, nebulous, speculative,
Challenging, confounding, but achievable.
Some students were loudly greeting other
Early arrivals in front of Teehan's, then
As they went inside, probably for a beer,
Silence. He fell asleep, smiling with his God.

The chapel permeated a protective warmth,
The evening sky gently backlighting the
Stained glass windows, blending them into
The shadows of the walls, which in turn
Were lost in the inky blackness under the
Beamed roof, where, it seemed, God himself
Spread his wings as he looked down, perhaps
Smiling, at his developing creation, kneeling,
Vainly trying to make contact with his Creator,
Knowing, as only faith can know, that somewhere
Above, his effort was recognized, an offering
Of future, a willingness to accept, not in
Submission, but to eagerly live the experience,
Prepared by the Master, of physical life.

* * *

The summer day had a cool glow, giving a
Crispness to the many hued greens bordering
The russet shadows of the glen. The other boys
Were discussing the rifle, but his attention went
To a chipmunk, playing in the leaves below.
He watched as it scurried through the leaves
Of the last fall, stopping to scratch at the
Ground, then rustling through a few feet to
A new discovery, giving a happy squeak as he
Worked to pry it loose, then held it in his paws,
nibbling, his small head bobbing rhythmically.
The rifle cracked, horrified, he saw the small
Animal jerk, fall on his back, and die.
"The sights are pretty good." The boy smiled.

* * *

Rumor had established the fact that Trinity girls
Were all looking for husbands. So they absented
Themselves from underclass mixers, except for a
Few freshmen. He paused at the top of the steps,
Flanked by his friends, studying the activity in
The smoke filled lounge. The band was playing
"Tenderly," the dance floor was full, and a group
Of girls standing on the side looked hopefully
From behind the safety of their cigarettes at the
Newcomers. Someone at his side said "Let's go in."

Later sociologists could classify it as "Culture Shock."
Eagerness covered by an incomplete veil of
Sophistication, a smile presenting an openness
Trembling with concern of form, wrong acceptance,
Rejection and peer status, overwhelming awareness
Of being—clearly focused in the minds eye standing
Apart, self observing self act, each movement
Rehearsed in dreams, catalogued for future need,
Recalled on cue and delivered, actor and audience
In one, critic and supporter, giver and receiver.

He didn't understand the "Where are you from—
Do you know who?" game. Was there a meaning in
Transfer? What could be added to a being by
Being from? Or by knowing who? A form of
Borrowed glory? Was there a reverse to the
"Sins of the father" concept, which enriched
The child? Even the foolish establishment
That Daddy never had to work—He drank himself
To death. Did it add or subtract a cubit
In the stature of the child? Perplexing.

* * *

Virtue

A forgotten word with forgotten meanings.
To accept reality as it is, creating truth as
A standard, allowing faith to act, hope to bolster
And love to radiate. Exercise prudence as a
Source of happiness against the corrosion of
Covetousness while justice supports love
In respecting reality's order. Bravery permits
Wounds, even death, in seeking the greater good,
Which is the essence of human nobility. And in
All, temperence acts as a monitor, avoiding
The destruction wrought by passion's fury.

The realm of wayward man has other virtues.
Reality is what I want to see, truth relative.
Faith has been raped by experience, hope
Eclipsed by prediction based in fact, and
Love darkened by fear. Prudence becomes
Selfishness, acquiring material for a rainy day,
While justice is a means of establishing
Material order. Bravery is an exercise in
Foolishness, since the ego is the greatest
Good, and temperence a measure of
Social acceptability.

With virtue's passing, romance becomes
A fiction. Excitement becomes only a
Physical thrill. The glory of enchantment
Is rendered to dull theory. Spirits no longer
Soar, but rather plod wearily through
The slough of Despond. The weight of
Man's physical concern separates him
Further from his spiritual source
As he spins in the Devil's centrifuge.

9/28/92

War Flair

For the good, it starts
Lest anyone think it evil;
For liberation, it continues
To reinforce the concept of liberty
In the mind of he who hears,
Lest the thought of having to sacrifice
Be considered an imposition;
For freedom, as if freedom can be given
Or won or experienced outside the soul;
For our friends, it concludes
Rainy day friends? A friend in need?
Yesterday's friend, Tomorrow's enemy;
Today's friend, Today's enemy?
The enemy of my enemy is my friend.

The judge called History laughs at
The follies played out on his stage.
The wise man is made a fool, and
The fool becomes sagacious.
Nation becomes Self,
Evil becomes Good,
Death without cause becomes Sacrifice,
Destruction renewal. Leaders push.

In the ripeness of time, Death is a friend
Who liberates the tried (but never tired) soul
From the often tired body, allowing escape to
The next experience. Yet it is reluctant to rip
Youth from the ordained physical pleasures
To be lived in this experience. The deprivation is
Obscenely Evil. Heroic sacrifice.

For what is glory? Does it substitute for the need
Individually required for the unfolding of the spirit
In the physical dimension? Perhaps a ripening agent?
And valor in a meaningless exercise? Is it valid to
Risk to save a common seed from a conflagration?
Games. Fanciful meanings. Foolishness.

So it is empty. A flawed vessel which allows life
To pour through its cracks, needlessly. Manipulated by
Wanton egos who would be historic, fearing their own
Meaninglessness. Seeking. Sneaking. Perverted.
Without flair.

1/9/91

THE LONELY MAN

The Lonely Man

Euphemism for he who cannot love, flawed,
Hurt, seeking himself in the hurt of others.
Crying out "Tell me who I am," yet
Closed to the answer, unable to see or
Feel beyond the aura of self, troubled,
Crippled, convoluted, trapped.

The infant ego, unpacked, wrapped in
Virginal self glory, failing the adult,
Searching for the warm breast, which is no more,
Or never was, with hysterical cries of hunger.

Alone, rejecting advances, unable to
Understand the giver, unknowing of that
Which is offered. Childlike in possession of
Things, to pull, to push, to take to bed,
To break.

Elusive love, created as it is given,
Impossible to be hidden away and treasured
In solitude, disappears as the mist before the wind,
Leaving the suffocating pain of the lung without air,
A collapsed void, unfillable through the
Weight of self pressing each space closed.

Until self is the only reality, and
Self clutches self ever more tightly in
Fear of losing. Until such time as
The Master allows the pained grasp to
Fatigue, and hesitantly release the grip.
Defeated and beaten, shamed, self collapses,
To be swept away by the Eternal Giver.

1/10/91

Metamorphosis

A word is the start, perhaps preceded by
A look. Effectively, nothing. Or something
Not understood. But felt somewhere deep in that
Which we call the soul. Our brain searches for
A meaning, sorting through impulses received over
Years, finding no match.

Is it the call of a soul, demanding its right of
Physical experience? Answered through the
Sympathy of other souls heeding the plan?

An uncontrollable force grows, a gravity futilely
Fought against, or gaily accepted, leading to
An explosive synergistic result. Parasitic perhaps.
But individual, rapidly undergoing within its
Cocoon the eonian activities of creation, to emerge
Separate, clothed in flesh, physically alive.

Initially dependent, immobile, instinctive, unaware,
Folded, it adapts. Eyes see, limbs straighten,
Effect recognizes cause as cause leads to effect.
Locomotion leads to exploration, exploration to
Knowledge. Or is knowledge released through activity?

Random knowledge gains pattern, the body grows,
And soon system develops, making knowledge usable.
Yet in the same instant the soul awakens, and in the
Throes of operating within a new existence, causes
Confusion, trying to contact the spiritual through
physical.

The unfilled knowledge system leads to wonderment, for
both
The soul about its physical experience, and the
Body about its newly awakened spirit. Innocence falls
Victim to knowledge, as wonder plunders reality. Yet
Each sunrise expands the need for new knowledge, until
In time, wonder flags, and the soul, having pity, calls
On Wisdom to show the reality of the spiritual.

Wisdom teaches wonder, and knowledge becomes its own
end,
Interesting in itself, harvest of the physical experience.
Perhaps to be brought by the soul as a souvenir to be
Gently laughed about in the warmth of hereafter.

1/14/91

INNOCENCE

Innocence

The questioning look may reveal its presence,
But the question goes unspoken, unformulated,
Since articulation is of this world, far from
The purity of the infant-child experience.
Since, for the child, everything is the way it is
Because it is. Unquestioned.

Good, better, best must be taught. Implying
Bad, worse, worst. Destroying innocence with
Knowledge. For it was no accident that
The tree was called the tree of knowledge.
He who knows cannot be innocent. So we have
The need to know. The need not to be innocent.

We are drawn to the child, in its sweetness,
Purity, simplicity, innocence. Yet, feel
Responsible to teach, show, instruct, offer
Experience, so the child will know. Help
Grow up. Or leave a more perfect state for one
Less perfect. Misery loving company.

Or is it that in return for the knowledge we give
We receive a like amount of innocence from the
Receiver? God's way of infusing innocence into
Our experience? The coin given to pay for a
Physical education for the spiritual? Or to keep
The scales in balance? For is there a greater
Truth than innocence?

1/15/91

TRUTH

Truth

The philosophers say truth is unity, yet
What is true for me may not be true for you.
So, truth is clarified, analyzed and
Categorized, leading to a multitude of truths
Each one, according to its definition.

Truth cannot be true and untrue at the same time.
But, what is true for me may not be true for you.
So, what is good may be evil, or evil good
Depending on where one stands. Or are good and
Evil absolutes? Or is evil the absence of good?
Can that which is absolutely good for me be less for you?

Absolute, relative, apparent. All good. All true.
Yet all different. We define God as good. God is
Truth. An absolute by definition. A measure, standard
By which a relative position can be determined.
Provided
One is in the God system. But one can reject the system.
Making the standard average. More true. Less true.
Appears to be more true, appears to be less true.

Or are the orientals more astute? Every being has its
Own truth. Nothing can be measured or compared.
Each
Being is its own universe. Yin and Yang. It is
What it is. All truth. Or no truth. So
What is true for me may not be true for you.

1/16/91

WAR MOOD

War Mood

As in preparing for a game, the attributes
Of each side are weighed, measured, discussed,
Compared and paired off, seeing if a prediction
Of the score can be more accurate. Camps of
Optimists and pessimists develop, each unthinking,
Yet sure in their thoughts.

For the thinker, the mood is different. Difference
In the natures of men, their beliefs, their experience
Seemingly cannot be compromised—in that there is
Sameness. So lacking compromise, a willing surrender
Of part, force is employed, preventing the gap,
Separating man from man, an increase in its dimension.
Man cannot live separate in lack of trust and respect,
So war supplies action for conviction, proving
Perhaps perversely, trust, and engendering respect.

Would that it be otherwise.

1/17/91

VISION

Vision

I gaze through the window, the field barren,
Broken only by frozen tufts of grass, violating
The smoothness of the snow, waiting as a screen
For a projection of a light image. Trancelike,
The mind reaches into the space that was, and forms
From nothing a hologram, dancing in the void
Between now and forever, filling the senses,
Suspended in time, with visions of that which
Never was, and may never be.

The girl-child, her eyes attentively focused,
Looking into the soul to make sure that she is
Carefully watched, gracefully awkward,
Performs her romantic ballet to the music of
The frost stilled forest. Intertwined
Flowers crown her hair, allowing nature to
Share for a moment, eternity, until nymphlike,
She vanishes into the ethereal background
Leaving a vacuum of empty wonderment.

1/22/91

Prayer

The clock strikes, measuring another segment of
Time, leaving us to ponder the vastness of
Eternity, searching for a meaningless meaning,
Beyond our finite grasp of apparentness.
We toy with each discovery, turning and twisting,
Trying to fit it into what we think is our
Puzzle, not comprehending the absurdity of
Our perceived intelligence.

For what is the value of being the greatest
Creature in creation, if in proving our
Position we denigrate the creator? And
What is the value of being the greatest
Among the greatest creatures?
Transient satisfaction to the immature mind.
Immersion into the small sphere to
Avoid the realization of impotence.

Wise men have noted the loss of the soul
Is not worth the gain of the world,
Instructing that there is no value relation
Between even one soul and the universe. Yet,
Is it not the soul itself which allows
Man to sacrifice it for material gain? Or
Is the soul powerless against free will?
Unable to bend man from choosing evil.

We do not understand the problem of evil.
The prince of darkness roams our world
Searching for souls which we call
Lost, lost in that their connection to
Their source has been flawed, and the
Source can no longer protect them. Or,
Free will has elected to go it alone,
Believing in humanistic powers to do.

Man craves immortality, yet in his frenzy
Foolishly attempts to preserve his essence
In the corruptible physical. Feeling he is
King of the universe, he ignores that power
Ordering the heavens, holding his feeble
Existence in His hand. Not realizing that
Immortality is contained in finding
Harmony with the creator.

And so it is that the pure souls, lacking
Complexity of physical awareness, in
Simple love raise their very essence in
Longing to return to their source,
Silently interceding with their prayer
Hoping He who is only known darkly, as
Through a mirror, will reach out and
Restore coherence to their kin.

1/29/91

Psalm

You are beyond all understanding, yet
Confident as I am in my knowledge
I seek to understand, not foolishly,
But perhaps in haste, wishing to
Obtain sight of you without having
To open the Door of Death.

My mind toys with the clues. You
Are present in the billions of
Whirling spheres, a physical display
Incomprehensible without the spirit of
Mathematics, itself a game we play to
Try and understand.

You are present in the dancing flow of
Water in a brook. I can let the smooth
Liquid glide coolly over my hand,
Feeling, still unable to know, since
As the water is formed by its container,
You can only be formed by my mind.

You are present in the song of a bird,
The laugh of a child, the sigh of a lover.
For a tantalizing moment you make a sound,
Then elude capture behind the veil of time.
I know you are there, leading me on
To seek you, lightheartedly, playfully.

Do I see you in the eyes of a hungry child?
Or is it me, my hunger for you, reflected
In those limpid dark pools? And other eyes
Reaching mine in a fleeting gaze from a crowd,
But held in my memory, perhaps forever, a
Window to something felt but not understood.

Your work is everywhere, simple beauty, yet
With complexity requiring generations of study
To reach minute comprehension, perhaps never to
Be understood, still beckoning the promise
Of finding you, or a concept of you
To be cherished as a valuable discovery.

As I grow wiser, I see the foolishness of my
Unrequited quest. There is no need to
Understand, for in understanding what is won?
Is your glory made more glorious? Does the sun
Shine brighter by knowing its source of light?
Is innocence purified by knowledge?

So I accept with joyous heart your gifts,
Unquestioning as to how or why, using them
As my nature directs, recognizing them as
Beyond my means of knowing, since if I could
Know, what then would be left to add
Purpose to our physical adventure?

1/31/91

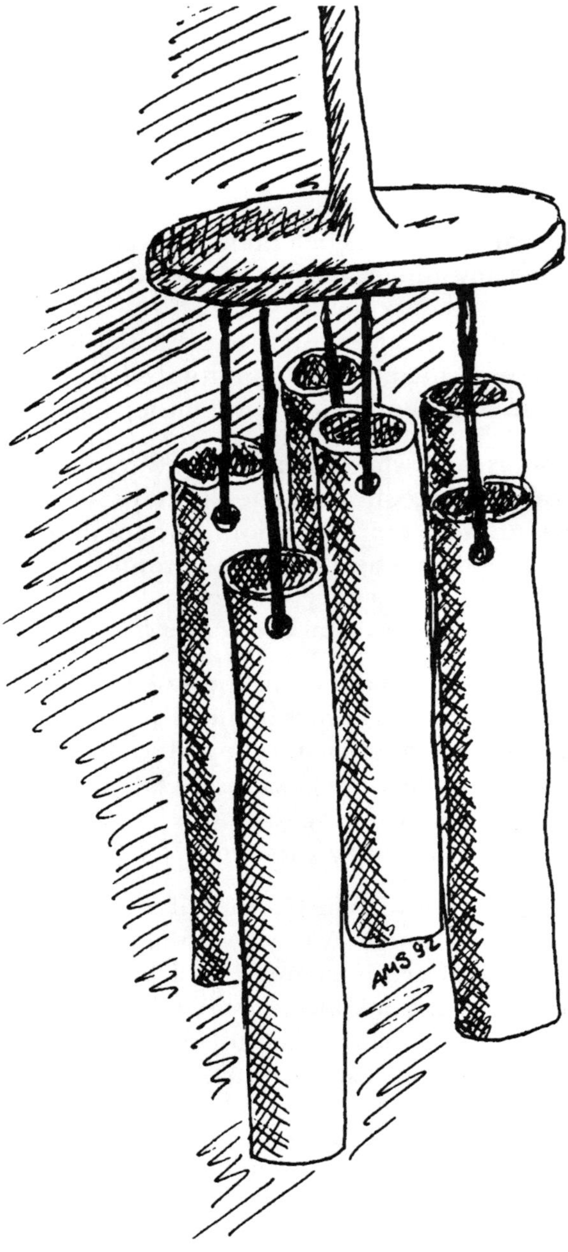

WIND CHIMES

Wind Chimes

The air is still except for the occasional
Eddy curling out from the woods, moving
Dead leaves from the past autumn in
Circles over the green emerging through
Protective dry stalks of last year's grass.

The stillness is broken as a gentle
Whisper of air breathes unobserved over
The landscape, passing as if by accident
The patient metal rods and hammer which
Strike the faint tone of distant cowbells.

Evoking thoughts of the high Himalayas;
Temples peopled by shorn priests; exotic
Foreign skies; a solitary tree; peace.
The gentle clink of the wind chime
God letting a pin drop.

2/5/91

MEMORIES

Memories

Like the tide they ebb and flow
They seem to swell up from below
Unexpected they can come and go
As the spring breeze might blow
While one seeks the fire's glow.

They seem separate at the start
Like something particularly set apart
In a special chamber of the heart
Then suddenly they deem to dart
To fit our mood a la carte.

2/5/91

REASON

Reason

As so many other words it is weak. Perhaps
Trying to cover too much. Blending logic with
Emotion. Why did you do it? I have my
Reasons. Motives? Causes? Sequence?
Are reasons reasonable? Based on flawed
Logic. Rational. Rationalized.

Why? Because. The child's answer. For a
Reason. A logical sequence which carries
Forward overcoming initial error, which is
Lost in the misting time affords. The Logic
Provides reason missing in the premise.
Form provides structure.

Truth. The basis of reason. But what is
True? If a straight line is not straight
In relativity, how do we define a point?
We hold this to be true. Definition. The
Starting point. If . . . Therefore.
Complicated by what if . . . then.

So we are forced to seek the ultimate
Truth. The uncaused cause. The
Unanswerable why. The indefinable
Definition. That which defies all
Reason. Yet which sequentially must
Have no beginning and no end. Is.

So reason to be perfect must start
In a plane where there is no start.
Reason functions in time, truth is
Timeless. Ergo, reason cannot be
Perfect. It strives for perfection
Pulling reluctant man to God.

2/6/91

TIME

Time

Time progresses. From before to after.
Before and after now. Does now exist?
Now is gone before we complete our thought,
Supplemented by a new now and another
And another, unending in its sequence.
Without respite, mindless, unstoppable.

Time does not exist, yet we measure it.
Year, month, week, day, hour, minute,
Second, nanosecond. Our mind gives it
Dimension. Our actions are measured
By it. Fast, slow, faster, slower.
Understandable, meaningful, felt.

Time is the medium of our lives. Our
language is crafted around it. Am,
Was, will be, would have been. To plan,
To remember, to act. To project and
Reflect. Expand and contract.
Begin, grow, age, die. Stop.

Time is the essence of continuity.
Yet apparent rates vary. For the
Young time is slow. For the old
Fast. In one life it accelerates.
In each life it accelerates, yet
Should remain constant. A given.

If time allows for motion, for
Accomplishment, is eternity
Motionless? Or motion transcending
Time? Or is time that physical
Necessity required in this plane
To prepare for the next? Eternal.

2/8/91

DESPAIR

Despair

The weight crushing, unrelenting,
Hopeless, squeezing the will into
Dead inaction. The sun does not
Thaw the freeze, but further torments
The mind, too fixed to confuse
With any glimmer of respite.

Despair follows want. True need or
Desire? Physical requirement for
Life, or imagined lack preventing
Recognition, fame, acceptance, love.
Blind, unable to recognize love, despair
Twists slowly, roped from a bough.

2/11/91

INFATUATION

Infatuation

They say it's fatuous love, love of
Form not substance. Yet love must have
A start, else it cannot grow. Is not
Every beginning fraught with
Foolishness, uncertainty, question,
Overcome by desire to possess?

Where does love start? A look, a
Touch, a word? Perhaps uncertain,
Certainly questioning. A calculated
Action hoping for a favorable reaction.
But as the biblical seed sown on rock,
Having small chance to flourish.

But blind desire gives way to Awareness;
Infatuation erodes into the medium where
Love takes root, fragilely at first,
Reinforced by recognition of the work
The mutual author presents as the
Compliment to each individual life.

2/12/91

TOMORROW

Tomorrow

Often it is the word of procrastination,
Lack of conviction, inaction, sloth.
Yet more often it is a statement of
Hope, faith in that which not yet is
Other than in the eye of God,
Preparation for what will be.

Tomorrow helps us through those
Barely bearable todays through which
Life tests endurance, will, even
Sanity, until rest arrives in its
Coach of darkness or exhaustion
Preparing us for our next today.

Tomorrow benefits from today's growth
In wisdom, in love, in overcoming.
Tomorrow we will have less innocence,
Unless we save it through faith,
Knowing today's activity prepares
Us for tomorrow's hopes.

2/14/91

DEATH

Death

My constant companion since birth, you
Protect me from an untimely
Separation from my body. You measure my
Physical needs and weakness, telling me my
Time is not yet ripe, so I continue
Life, accepting your judgment.

You make my time in time one of joy,
Teaching me the value of my physical
Experience yet promising, when joy ceases,
An end, when you will take me, carefully,
To that place beyond the sunset, where
Spiritual delights abound eternally.

2/20/91

MEDITATION

Meditation

All is confusion except within, where
Stillness reigns, forcing silence to
Permeate from the core of being as
Light from a beacon, giving direction.
Calling senses to it, they are made
Numb with the pressure of its fire.

The mind reaches out to that nowhere
Beyond where the stars gently swim
In the nothingness of the heavens,
Probing for the answer to an unasked
Question, unknowingly seeking as a
Baby seeks its mother's breast.

That which the mind seeks to avoid
Consciously, filling itself with
Problems of little consequence, is
Sought in the quiet moments when the
Soul takes control, directing the mind to
Search for the ultimate cause.

The liquid wind of divinity washes the
Mind with its soothing coolness,
Returning it to its paradisiac state,
Easing it, strengthened, into the
Stream of consciousness to radiate
Love beyond all understanding.

2/21/91

My Love

To me you were a little girl, dressed to
Go out, out to where you knew not what
Waited, and what you met was your
Future. I saw you, graceful as a
Willow, alert as a child on Christmas,
Yet soft as a night breeze in summer.

I held you as we danced, perhaps with the
Elation of possession common to the young,
But deep in my being something smiled, knowing
The hectic search was now satisfied,
Years of trial, blind alleys, apparent
Meaning overcome, life starting for real.

What is this wonderful eye which can
See where there is nothing to ascertain,
Project into the soul and know its
Direction, when the soul itself has
Kept its direction secret? Do
Souls speak to each other?

Opposites attract, yet conflict in their
Being, since thereby are they opposite.
If conflict can be avoided, they are
Complementary, each filling the void
Found in the other, and so doing become
One, complete and fulfilled, at rest.

How does love work? It allows the
Fascination found in difference, an
Awe in watching a performance which
Contradicts the direction of the ego,
Without frustration, without interference,
Without doubt, without pain, with trust.

Trust grows, fascination remains, awe
Becomes delight, new worlds open exposing
Beauties never realized earlier in the
Days of half-being. Every crevice of
Life is permeated with warm contentment,
Expanding, secure, peaceful, loving.

And the little girl lives on, still
Surprising, coy, playful, enchanting.
Beauty enhanced by the response to the
Vagaries of life, a world in convolution,
Seeking good to be dispensed with love
Finding God in a child.

3/4/91

DREAM

Dream

Reality on another plane, tireless action
Felt, lived, remembered, forgotten,
Blending into experience as threads
Woven into a pattern of fantasy, to be
Admired, thought about, then discarded,
Minus an essence, spiritually absorbed.

A timeless projection, bringing past and
Future together, that which was, may be,
Might have been. Corrector of folly, or
Indulgent creator of joy without consequence,
Fear without disgrace, passion without
Shame, love from the secretly loved.

Perhaps it is the true reality, the
Sleeping thought of another being, calling
To be that which is our existence, even
Ourselves, to live on the landscape of
Is, a now which can forever disappear,
With us, as the day brings wakefulness.

3/7/91

WISHES

Wishes

Night comes, filling blackness from the
Deepest crevices as ink rising in a
Reservoir, engulfing finally the ethereal
Void, erasing care, negating reality.
The moon's silver brightens, to be
Joined coyly by the first star.

Through the window, marginally frosted,
The star appears to the child in its
Bed, protected by prayer, strengthened
By having to protect the tightly clutched
Doll, companion for the journey through
Sleep, confidant of dreams and wishes.

The wish of a child is the wish of God.
Innocent, simple, healing, loving,
Lacking gain, restoring harmony. From
The wish comes the dream, giving the
Child unencumbered access to God.
Star light, star bright, first star.

3/18/91

Longing

Can it be described, that void within,
Ripping at being, clawing to pull the
Walls to fill the center, yet unable
To satisfy the gnawing hunger which
Burns, unabated, expanding the nothingness
To all encompassing empty pain.

Without you, living is a meaningless
Masquerade, a facade of engagements,
Contrived duties, empty talk, foolishness.
Inside, my soul searches for you,
Calling with passion, wearying as
Echoes reply, futile, cold, hollow.

My mind conjures up your face, your
Body, giving respite to my pain, which
Returns with fury as the vision returns
To mist, gently smiling as it fades,
Beckoning, until my very heart
Cries to its creator for pity.

You return, walking slowly towards me;
Down a street glistening in the rain,
Reflecting the night light of the
City; stepping carefully to avoid a
Puddle, then looking up at me, only
To disappear as the drops of rain.

Your image taunts me, I follow you on
My walk, then you turn and look at me
Through the eyes of another, unknown,
Wondering, amused by the appearance of
This stranger's anticipation then
Disappointment, abysmal longing.

Why must we be apart, what reason can
Exist that would compensate for the
Pain? What is the unknown crime
Demanding this punishment? Or do I cry
For a you which never was, an apparition
Fleetingly enfolded, then forever gone.

3/19/91

SWING

Swing

The delightful look of anticipation
Flashes as she is slowly pulled backwards,
Higher then her feet can reach,
Her hands gently grasping the chains
Which will support her flight, freeing
Her from the mysterious cares of childhood.

"Higher, Granddaddy, higher than I've ever
Been before," she pleads, applying a
Childlike logic to a problem long lost
To the confusion of pseudological values
Burdening the adult mind. "Still higher,
So I can go to the top of the trees."

With a squeal of pleasure she greets the
Release, and arcs downward, then out and
Up, blonde hair streaming behind, relaxed,
Observant, soaking up the freedom of space,
Exchanging thoughts with the distant mountains,
Pondering feelings felt but forgotten.

She returns to earth, leaving her heavenly
Chariot, and runs off, refreshed, satisfied,
Having experienced the wind of eternity, to
Engage in the joy of being. Knowing that
When the trees and sky beckon, access
Hangs waiting in the form of a swing.

4/10/91

Mind Game

Snow in July. Sheep misled by the
Shepherd. Non comprehension of that
Which is self evident. Inability to
Surmount the plane for the mountain of
Convention. Restriction by making
Right wrong. Debilitation by taboo.

If free will makes man man, why
Confuse and pervert through should
And should not? Do and don't?
Is not every will capable of measuring
Consequence? For good and evil.
My good and my evil.

But what of you? Can I seek my good
In your evil? Or your good in my evil?
Can good be evil? Or is evil in the mind
Of the observer, making good evil. Or
Does evil only exist in the mind of the
Manipulator, bending good to control?

If we would be as God, love would be limitless.
As God made all things good, we created
Evil in our frustration of attaining perfection.
Wanting to be as God, we destroyed
Innocence. Corrupted love to provide
Power. Selfish, jealous, measured.

The child's mind is trained to limit.
Love not all mothers. Nor all fathers.
Mommie. Daddy. To trust is to risk.
Love has boundaries. Don't waste it on
Those not worthy. Don't wear
Your heart on your sleeve.

So life becomes a mind game. I think
Therefore I am. I love, but only in my
Mind. My soul can reach out and touch
Other souls, comforting them as they need.
My body, prisoner of law, abider of
Convention, stays writhing in bondage.

4/22/91

INTERLUDE

Interlude

A moment in time, a dream made
Incarnate, a fantasy lived, suddenly
Awakened, reluctantly put to sleep,
Recurring as a vision in the
Evening sky as the failing sun rays
Caress the clouds of night.

But a scene in an act in the
Play of life, a crossing of characters,
Travelling from opposite ends of a
Fog bound sea, suddenly viewing the
Moon through a break in the mist, then
Separating, submerging in life's flow.

A lingering longing confuses the
Senses, trying to recognize that which
Was from that which might have been,
Reality from desire, the warp in time's
Order, bending to whisper feelings
Only touched by the wind.

6/13/91

BITTERSWEET

Bittersweet

Sweet, yet with the contrasting pang of
Discomfort, aborted love reminisced, the
"If" of life to be turned in wonderment,
Projecting scenarios of never to be, still
Reflected upon as an existing reality. For
Love, once lived, only passes, never dies.

The touch, the smile, the meeting of glances,
The radiation received and returned, were,
And the sensation remains stored in the
Memory, indelible, to be recalled in those
Moments between wakefulness and sleep,
When the bitter mingles with the sweet.

Perhaps, in dreams dreamt separately, the
Love is fulfilled, lived on a plane removed
From our cares, nearer the source, where,
After our adventure in the physical, we
Relive that which might have been, but was,
Unknown to our ego filled singularity.

7/8/91

TO A SLEEPING CHILD

To a sleeping child

You sleep, your cheeks still rosy
From the excitement of another day's
Discoveries, your eyelids slightly
Quivering as you digest existence,
Unencumbered by questions unanswerable,
Secure in the hand of God.

Do you reflect on the cares of life?
The sad smile of a mother no longer loved
The clouded face of a father, not
Understanding, yet misunderstood?
Subtle anger, eroding the ground around
The roots which support your being.

In the day your glances probe the mist
Surrounding your pillars of protection,
And you see the rift widening into an
Abyss, yet innocence protects you with
Its power to cover the encroaching
Evil, blocking the incomprehensible.

So you sleep, as those who should preserve
Your innocence allow love to be
Corroded, instance by instance, until
It is consumed, leaving the repulsive
Feces of hate, for you to observe,
Gaining experience, losing beauty.

You smile, perhaps your dream created
A new delight, synthesizing your waking
Observations. Your head turns ever so
Slightly, perhaps grazed by the wings
Of your guardian angel, fluttering close
Telling you of eternal love.

7/9/91

Summer

In early morning the sun cracks over
The mountain, its burnished light
Reflected from the leaves of the
Maple and oak, changing as the
Rolling sea, constant as the
Fungi speckled rock.

Warblers, jays and sparrows flit
Furtively among the trees as the
Robin paces the newly cut field,
All searching for a morsel found
Attractive, while the crickets
Creak to welcome the warmth.

The crispness of morning fades
To the languid smoothness of day,
The heat distilling the essence of
Earth and plant, delicious to
Breathe, wafted by the occasional
Breeze, penetrating the soul.

The spring rush of the brook
Is stilled, water seeps now from
Pool to pool, still cool in the
Shadows of its canopy of trees,
While water striders walk and dart
Mysteriously on its surface.

Late afternoon the sky becomes
Painted with clouds, silently appearing
Preparing for the waning heat
Of evening, when, after sunset
Heat lightning bubbles burst behind
Black dreadnoughts on the sea of night.

Visions of summers past swim slowly
Through the mind. The glow of a
Fathers cigarette, the smile of a
Summer's love, the holiday burst of
Fireworks, the gently flapping sails
Of a boat rocking at its mooring.

In the seasons of man, representative
Of the fullness of life, ripening of
The grown child, realization of love,
Contentment and harmony. A foretaste
Of that which beckons on that
Dawning of the last day.

7/10/91

HARVEST MOON

Harvest Moon

The soothing warmth of the day is
Cut short by the early twilight,
Glorious in its dark crimson glow
Radiating from behind the distant
Mountains, dark and brooding,
Mourning the loss of their short-lived
Flamboyantly colored cover. The
Evening sounds have changed from
Gentle soft leave rustlings to the
Scrape of death, wind-blown over rocks,
Guarded by the gaunt grey procreators,
Bending to and fro, exchanging memories.

You peek over the crest, as if assuring
Yourself all traces of day have vanished,
Then in ever increasing speed overwhelm
The mountain, making it appear small as
You leap skyward, bringing a new life to
The devastation of change, illuminating
Death, allowing us in our finitude to
See, in a world of black and silver,
Manifestations of glory, stripped as
By X-ray of superficial distraction,
Of He who made both the day and the
Night, light and dark, life and death.

10/24/91

THE FOOL

The Fool

How is it you walk with such direction,
Your ill fitting clothes, unfashionable,
Covering your lanky being as a tarp
Sheltering a woodpile, each ungainly
Angle attracting attention as you move,
Surpassed only, perhaps, by your plodding
Feet, oversized, plopping directionless
As you proceed, eyes bulging with intent,
Mouth grinning, in satisfied anticipation
Of an attainable pleasure, unseen by me?

I watch as heads shake and knowing glances
Are exchanged, smug thoughts secretly shared
Anchored in certainty born of convention,
Judgments based on the reality of knowing,
Knowledge tempered by experience,
Worldly, successfully applied,
Reasonable, sure, proven, closed.
Still, an element of fear, a weighing
Of possibilities, a distrust, a
Disappointment of a system gone wrong.

Are you a dumb messenger, a stimulus
To reopen our minds? Subtle, penetrating
The alert consciousness silently,
Causing wonder at your actions, a
Musing at the unencumbered passage
You seem to enjoy, a bafflement at
Innocence preserved, the childlike
Acceptance of our worldly confusion,
An example to be added to the equation,
To balance the problem posed by God?

10/30/91

FANTASY

Fantasy

Your image leaps out at me, your smile
Inviting, your eyes playing with my soul,
Your body, naked in the night, tantalizing
My senses into a frenzy of desire, driving
Them to the edge of rapacity, bringing life
To the thought, experiencing the engulfing
Thrill of ravishing and being ravished,
Consuming and being consumed. Primeval
Sounds rush from your throat as you strain
To pivot your being on mine, as I silently
Thrust, seeking the core of your existance,
Probing with all my power to overcome the
Physical barrier keeping us two, then in
A flash we unite, radiant, exhausted.

Do you really exist, or have I made you,
Piecing together reality and dream,
Discarding that which is less than perfect,
Enhancing perfection with a thousand
Bits of memory, collected as so many
Wisps of dust over time stretching back
To the mist of life's beginning, when
He saw what He made was good? Were our
Souls, nay, are our souls entwined as my
Mind depicts, programmed to communicate
Forevermore, signaling across the ether,
Awakening hungers, bringing solace,
Questioning, demanding, doubting,
Living separately together in fantasy?

11/7/91

WOMAN

Woman

Do not lose that which makes you unique
In creation, your mystery, your love,
Your softness; cradling hope in your
Heart, while you measure reality with
Your mind, applying your being to
Bridge the abyss between the two,
Subtly, impetuously patient,
Instinctive, methodically emotional.

You passionately embrace living from
Conception to wake, when you feel loss,
Undefined, undeserved, punishing, yet
Absorbing the pain, you turn to the
Living, to console, to comfort, to
Nurture, for that is your gift to
Our race. While others philosophize,
You act, for you life is to be lived.

11/8/91

You embrace your man, filling his
Crevices, making him whole, yet
Retaining your wholeness, growing
In all aspects of your being,
Thriving through your gift of
Sustaining life, learning while
Teaching, conquering while
Praying, one with reality.

11/15/91

WHIMSY

Whimsy

Does it exist, as the fairy tales
Suppose, somewhere in that space
East of the Sun and West of the Moon?
Where magic skis carry handsome Princes
Clad in silks and fur across snowy wastes
To rescue Beautiful Princesses held in
Labyrinthine prisons by heartless ogres
Waiting for a blood moon to proclaim
Time for their feast of living innocence?
Where virgin princesses renounce kingdoms
For the love of a simple keeper of sheep.
Or is it nothing more than a wisp of whimsy?

Crystal caves mysteriously illuminated
Opening on icy underground lakes, transparant
To the treasures resting on their bottom,
Transversed by dragon shaped vessels
Piloted by liveried mice, transporting
Fruits and sweets to delight the taste
While in the hushed cavern etherial
Music gently harmonizes the echo of
Water, dropping drop by drop, pinging
The lake's surface, the shore reflecting
The wave disturbance, a ripple of real
In a world rejected by reality.

12/31/91

LUCIFER

Lucifer

Should I pity you, fallen Angel?
Was your anger caused by not being
Allowed to share in the physical?
Deprivation of experience and
Thereby knowledge?

Does your lust for the sensual cause you
To try and confuse our souls into forgetting
The balance required to see God? Or
Are you innocent, not able to control your emotion
For that which was created for Man alone?

Or is it vicarious satisfaction you seek?
By causing the soul lost in the carnality of life
To be forfeited to your kingdom where
You can revel together perhaps reliving the
Animal passions consumed in burying
The spiritual essence of our beings?

Maybe you are allowed to wander on our plane
As a reminder to us of the limits
We must place on excess. Respected
As an enemy lying in ambush,
Luring with material glitter, to be repulsed
By recognition of our satiety.

You should not envy Man.
Each of us has our place in
The plan. Every gift has its
Reward or loss, contingent
On its application. What have
You won by rejection? Rejection.

9/16/92

NIGHT

Night

A chill passes through my being
As the golden glow of the sun
Fades from the sky behind the
Purple mountain wall to the west.
Behind me stands the night,
Slowly wrapping its black cloak
Around me, like a mother carefully
Covering a child to protect it, from
That evil which only a mother knows.
The wind stills, perched breathless
On the treetops, poised, listening
As for a command, silent, watchful
Absorbing sound, working with night
To create nothingness, pure, ethereal,
Penetrating, timeless, eternity.

9/25/92